Contents

A Perfect Zoo?	2
Zoo Chat	10
Grand Theft Koala	16
A Giraffe's Best Friend	26

Old zoo exhibits

A Perfect

Written by P. J. Carling

Hundreds of years ago,
zoos kept their animals in cages.
The floors were cold and hard.
Often the animals
had nowhere to hide or sleep.

Many zoo animals were bored and unhappy.
Some stopped having babies.
Some even died!

Modern zoo exhibits

Zoo?

Today, zoos have changed. Most zoos try very hard to make their animals feel at home. They keep the animals in exhibits that look and feel just like the wild.

An exhibit (ig ZI bit) is the place where a zoo animal lives.

It's not easy to make a good zoo exhibit.
Zoo designers have to learn
all about the animals.
Some even go to see
the animals living in the wild.

The designers decide how
the exhibit should look.
Then they put together
a team of people
to build the exhibit.

A jungle exhibit being built

The designers want the exhibit to look like nature. But not everything is natural. The builders might make trees out of concrete. They might make vines out of rubber. They paint them to look real.

Artificial plants such as these can be used in any climate. And they don't need any care.

What other materials could zoo designers use to make an exhibit look real?

Painting "fungus" onto a concrete "tree"

Design a Zoo Exhibit!

Choose an animal you want to make an exhibit for. Learn as much as you can about your animal. How and where does it live?

My animal: Jaguar
Habitat: Rain forest

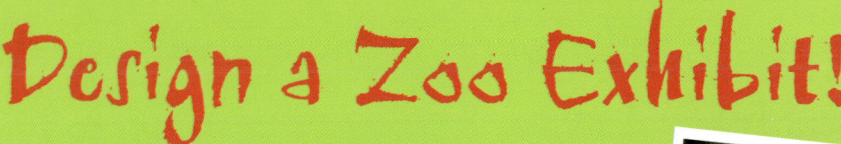

Does a _jaguar_ like…

to live with others? — No
a quiet place to sleep? — Yes
to live near water? — Yes
a place to climb or dig? — Climb
hot or cold weather? — Hot

Now think about your exhibit. How can you keep the animal, the people, and the zookeepers safe and happy? How can you make your animal really feel at home?

- Curved path for privacy
- Hidden door for keeper
- Speakers that play sounds of the rain forest
- Interesting signs

ZOO CHAT

Written by Sharon Griggins

BluBoy: Tomorrow is my class trip to the zoo. :-) I can't wait!!!

Mika_grrl: YUCK! I don't like zoos. I hate seeing animals in cages. :-(

Nicki3: What are you talking about? Zoos are good places for animals.

Mika_grrl: Wild animals belong in the wild. Even the best zoo isn't like an animal's real home.

BluBoy: But most zoos have really good exhibits. They look like the wild. The animals probably do feel at home.

Post Reply

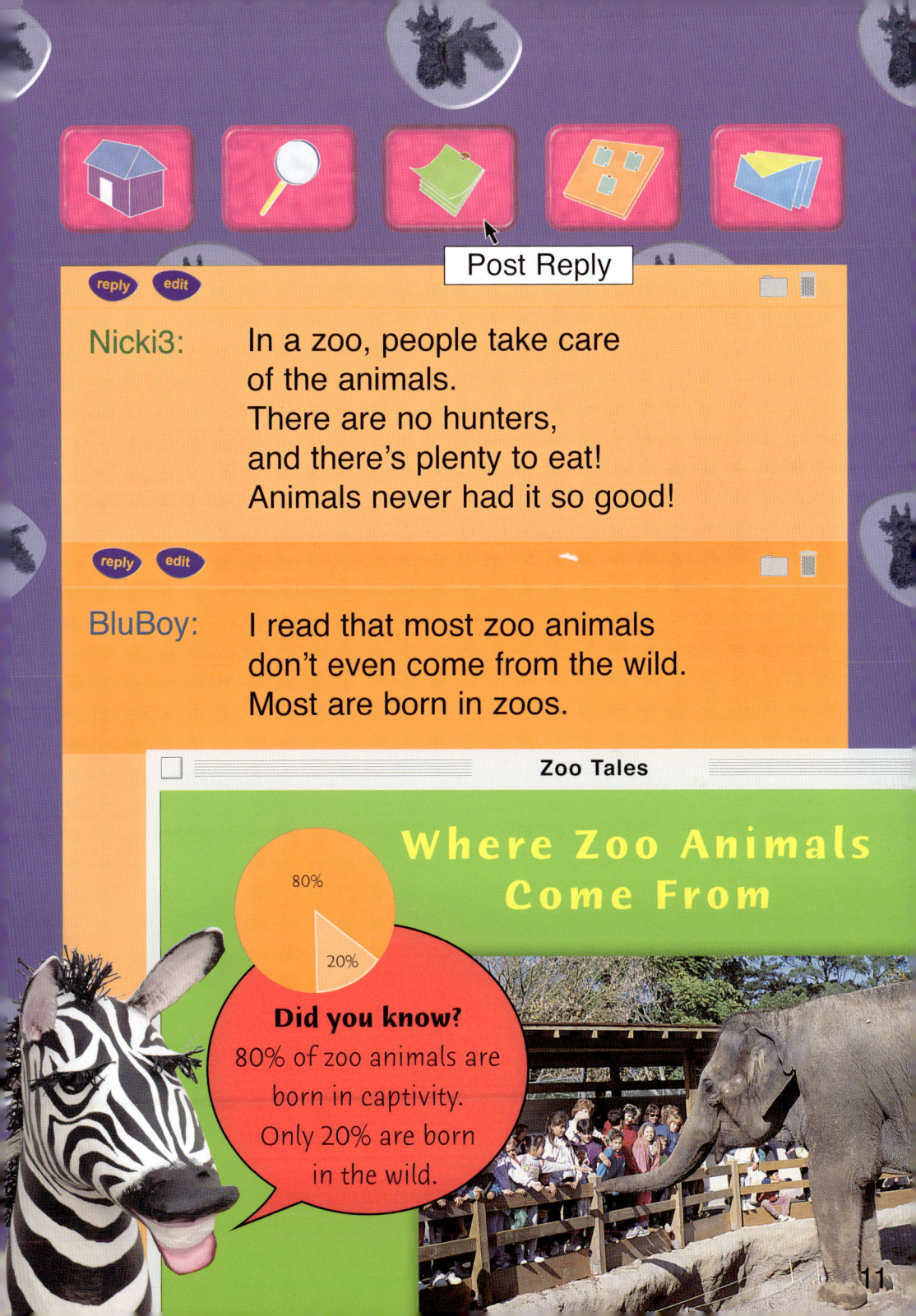

Nicki3: In a zoo, people take care of the animals. There are no hunters, and there's plenty to eat! Animals never had it so good!

BluBoy: I read that most zoo animals don't even come from the wild. Most are born in zoos.

Zoo Tales

Where Zoo Animals Come From

80%
20%

Did you know? 80% of zoo animals are born in captivity. Only 20% are born in the wild.

Search

Omar911: But, in zoos, animals have sad lives. :-(
Sometimes, they have to live
in a place that's too hot for them.
Sometimes, they have to live
in a place that's too cold.

Mika_grrl: RIGHT!!!!
Think about a polar bear
living in Australia!

Omar911: And, for most animals,
a zoo is too small.
Wolves walk for miles in the wild.
They can't do that in a zoo.

Mika_grrl: Animals hate being
in the same space day after day.
They get bored. <sad sigh>

Zoo Tales

POLAR BEAR: GUS

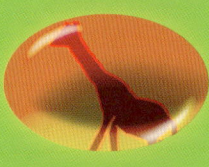

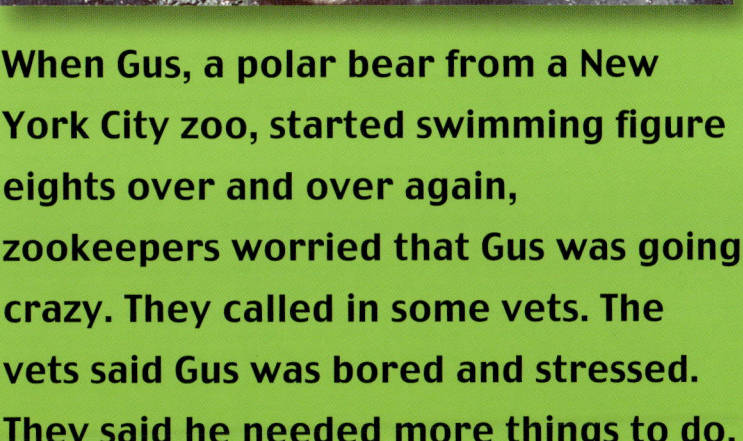

When Gus, a polar bear from a New York City zoo, started swimming figure eights over and over again, zookeepers worried that Gus was going crazy. They called in some vets. The vets said Gus was bored and stressed. They said he needed more things to do.

Post New Topic

BluBoy: How do you know what an animal feels?

Nicki3: Wild animals are losing their homes as people build houses where animals live.

BluBoy: Some species of animals are dying out. Zoos take care of rare animals. Sometimes, zoos return these rare animals to the wild. Without zoos, these animals would be extinct.

What do you think? Should animals be kept in zoos?

Zoo Tales

Saving Animals in Danger

Zoos have saved animals such as the California condor. By the mid-1980s, there were no more condors left in the wild, but zoos had been breeding and raising condors in captivity. More than 10 years later, some condors were released into the wild and are now free again.

Omar911: Come on.
Zoos are made for people, not animals.
People go to zoos for fun.

Mika_grrl: Zoos make money $$
by keeping wild animals for us to see.
That's not right. :-(
Wild animals should be free.

Grand Theft Koala

Written by Terry Miller Shannon
Illustrated by Craig Smith

Koalas at Sunville Zoo

mystery casebook
This ~~journal~~ belongs to:
Max

November 26

Karma's <u>really</u> mad
and, for once, it's not at me.
What was Ben thinking?
He should know that
boyfriends should **never**
forget birthday presents.
Especially when that present is for Karma!
I'm only Karma's brother,
and I know better than that.
I wonder what he will do?

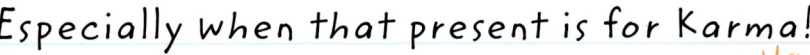

> How do you think a friend would feel if you forgot their birthday?

November 27

Karma's crying her eyes out,
but this time it's not because of Ben.
Some idiot broke into the zoo
and **stole two koalas** (koe AH lehz)!
Karma really likes those koalas.
She visited them all the time.
I wish I could catch the thief.
Then I would be a **hero**!

KOALAS STOLEN!

November 27, afternoon

When Ben came over to pick up Karma, he told me he had a **huge** surprise for her.

"It's a secret," Ben said. "But your sister will love her late birthday present!"

I wonder what it could be? Ben is acting really **weird**.

Ben's jacket had a strange smell. Maybe it's from the present? Could this be a clue?

November 27, later

When Ben brought Karma home,
she ran straight up to her room.
She won't come out,
and she won't tell anyone
what is wrong.
She's <u>storming</u> mad.
I've never seen her like this.
Something **strange** is going on.

Karma

Ben

Me with my spy camera

From my spy camera

November 27, evening

When I went to tell Karma to come down for dinner, she was on the computer. She tried to hide the screen, but I couldn't help seeing that she was reading about koalas. What is going on?

What do you think Max is going to discover?

Koalas are not bears! They are related to kangaroos. A baby koala rides in its mother's pouch.

November 27, after dinner

I just heard Karma on the phone.

"Take them back, Ben," she said.
"They could die!"

And now, suddenly, I know.
Ben has stolen the koalas!
But what should I do?

Thief!

November 27, late at night

I can't sleep.
Karma would hate me if I called the police.
But this is <u>important!</u>
I read about koalas on the Internet.
They need special food and a home that's kept at the right temperature. 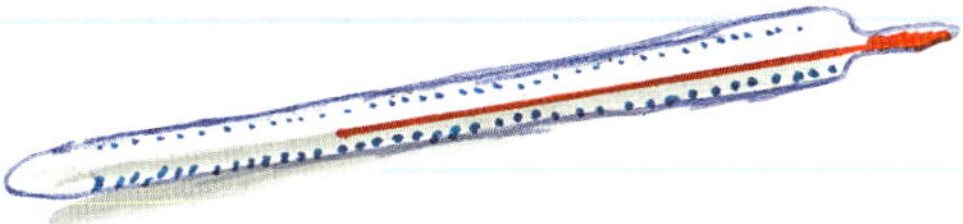
They could **die** soon without the right care.

Koala food doesn't come in cans!

Koalas are very picky eaters. They only eat the freshest eucalyptus (yoo kuh LIP tuhs) leaves. They also need a warm, controlled climate.

November 28, early morning

I crept out to the kitchen.
I went over to the phone.

"Max," said a voice out of the darkness.

I almost died.
I flicked on the lights.
It was only Karma.

"I rang the police," she said.
"I told them Ben's got the koalas."

Karma sounded sad,
but at least she didn't sound angry any more.

Police officer

November 28, afternoon

Ben's in **big trouble** now! The koalas will probably be OK. They were hungry, thirsty, tired, and scared, but now they're eating and resting. Karma is really glad the koalas are safe, and so am I. I didn't get to be a hero. But Karma is my **hero** for doing the right thing.

KOALAS COME HOME!

In 2000, two boys stole two koalas from San Francisco Zoo. They tried to give them as gifts to their girlfriends, but they wouldn't take them. Someone rang the police the next day. The koalas went back to the zoo. The boys were arrested. No one knows who rang the police.

"Grand Theft Koala" was inspired by these events, but our characters and story are entirely fictional.

A Giraffe's Best Friend

Written by Sharon Griggins

Suzie is a zookeeper.
She takes care of giraffes.

 **Q:** What is your day like?

 A: In the morning, I count my animals.
I look to see whether any of them are sick.
I put out their food.
I let them into their outdoor exhibit.
Next, I have to clean their indoor home.
In the afternoon, I put out their dinner.
I put down their straw bedding.
When the zoo closes,
I bring the animals inside for the night.

Suzie is preparing some food for her giraffes.

The giraffes are very curious. They like to see what Suzie is doing.

 What is the hardest part of your job?

 Cleaning a big giraffe barn
is hard work!
You have to be very strong.
You have to lift heavy hay
and pick up dung.
You have to work outside all day,
in sunshine or rain.

 **Q:** What's the funniest thing that ever happened at work?

 A: One of my giraffes had a crush on me!
His name was Rafiki.
When he saw me,
he would run over and lick my face.
He would follow me around.
For some reason,
I was special to him.
I was like
his best friend.

> Giraffes' tongues are 45 to 50 centimetres long! How would you feel if that tongue licked your face?

 What makes a good zookeeper?

 Zookeepers have to be very aware of what is happening to their animals. Animals can't tell you when they are sick. You have to watch how they act. Are they eating the way they normally do? Are they moving the way they normally do? Keepers also need to be careful. An animal's whole life depends on your care.

Giraffes and zebras live together in the wild. Sometimes, they live together at the zoo, too!

It's also part of Suzie's job to teach people about giraffes. If people can learn to care about giraffes as much as Suzie does, then giraffes will always have people to keep them safe in the future.

Index

artificial	5, 8–9	koalas	16, 18, 21–25
bored animals	2, 12–13	nature	5
cages	2, 10	polar bears	12–13
California condor	15	Gus	13
climate	5, 8, 23	sick animals	30
endangered animals	14–15	vets	13
eucalyptus leaves	23		
exhibits	3–9, 10, 27	wild	3, 4, 10–12, 14–15, 30
giraffes	26–31	wolves	12
tongues	29	zebras	30
home	10, 14, 27	zoo designers	4–5
hunters	11	zookeepers	7, 8, 13, 26–31
jaguar	6–9	Suzie	26–31